MAPS & DESTINATIONS
new and selected poems

Mary K. Stillwell

STEPHEN F. AUSTIN STATE UNIVERSITY PRESS
NACOGDOCHES ★ TEXAS

Library of Congress Cataloguing-in-Publication Data
Stillwell, Mary K.
        Maps & Destinations / Mary K. Stillwell
        ISBN: 978-1-62288-057-7
1. Life—Relationships—Family—United States—Poetry.
3. Title.

Book design by Andrea Laham and Kirstie Linstrom

Manufactured in the United States of America

Stephen F. Austin University Press
P.O. Box 13007 SFA Station
Nacogdoches, TX 75962
sfasu.edu/sfapress
sfapress@sfasu.edu

For Frank

Why is love beyond all measure of other human possibilities so rich and such a sweet burden for the one who has been struck by it? Because we change ourselves into that which we love, and yet remain ourselves. Then we would like to thank the beloved, but find nothing that would do it adequately. We can only be thankful to ourselves. Love transforms gratitude into faithfulness to ourselves and into an unconditional faith in the Other. Thus love steadily expands its most intimate secret.

—Martin Heidegger

Acknowledgments

Billingham Review, "Piano Four Hands"

Confrontation, "In the Morning in Morocco"

Cooweescoopwee, "The Florence Home"

The Crack in the Air: Poems from the Prairie (anthology),
"Fallen Angels" and "The Tourist"

Earth's Daughters, #33/34, "Daylilies"

Fine Lines, "A Waltz for my Mother"

Hurākan, "This Is the Way It Is."

Literal Latte, "Circle Dance"

The Little Magazine, "The Night the Monsky-Lewis Showroom
Burned Down"

The Massachusetts Review, "The Three Sisters"

Nimrod, "*Waiting*"

The Paris Review, "The Cutting," "Love Poem," and "Travel
Plans"

The Untidy Season (anthology), "Black Cardinal" and "Harvest"

South Dakota Review, "The Letter" and "Lavender Sweet Peas"

Sou'wester, "The Apartment"

"Travel Plans" subsequently appeared in *The Paris Review Anthology* (Norton) and "Circle Dance" also appeared in *Times of Sorrow/Times of Grace* (Houghton Mifflin), *Crazy Woman Creek* (Backwaters Press), and *Nebraska Presence* (Backwaters Press).

The following poems were collected in *Moving to Malibu*, Sandhills Press, Ord, NE: "The Visitation," "In the Morning in Morocco," "The Night the Monsky-Lewis Showroom Burned Down," "The Three Sisters," "This is Brooklyn," "Not Necessarily Based on my Father's Description" (published as "To Adele"), "The Cutting," "Love Poem," and "*Waiting.*"

The following poems were collected in *Fallen Angels*, Finishing Line Press, Georgetown, KY: "*Dialog with Space*," "In the Morning in Morocco," "Marrakesh," "The Tourist," "Grave Rubbing," "*Woman with a Balance*," "*The Art of Painting*," "*The Little Street*," "Sometimes I Imagine How It Might Be," "Moving to Malibu," "*Waiting,*" "Daylilies," "Travel," "After Sightseeing," and "*Mountain Figure.*"

CONTENTS

DEPARTURES

The Florence Home

Even today it's a white barn
of a building, an apartment house
so square and sturdy you'd think
it was raised by Amish in a single
day; the broad-brimmed flood light,
ringed planet against a winter sky,
shines bright over the double doors.

Accompanied by a friend
or maybe alone, late summer
—grass full and green, leaves
thick and heavy on the maple—
she walked up the hill
where the road seemed to end;
when she climbed all the way,
she saw it didn't.

THE APARTMENT

After my mother stole me, she struck
the earth so it would open
and carried me underground
where pipes thumped and squealed,
and summer was just about over.

Worms did the hokey-pokey
and turned themselves around;
water bugs shimmied up the drains.

Grandmother's lips were as thin
as a razor; lullabies bled to death.
Grandfather slipped inside a shaft
of light at the top of the stairs,
and, quick as a card trick, disappeared.

In the early months, it was night
and, eventually, winter. Miles away
the river whispered, *Time
to get going.* Nights got longer,
the shovel scraped hard against
the coal bin floor; dust hung in the air.

Rhizomes and bulbs resting on the other
side of the wall counseled,
Warm weather's coming; hang on.
When cars splashed by, the odor
of kerosene street lanterns curled
under the door. When I stumbled
on a skull, my fingers sought handholds.

Spring! Mother, taking courage, carried

me to the surface where the lilac thrust
its lavender fists skyward. Time passed.
I donned the ruffled skirts of the hollyhock,
confetti from the bushes flecked my hair.

LOVE POEM

for my grandfather

Riding in the wake
of your electric shock,
I was your therapy.
You pushed my plastic
carriage through the winter
with long, crazy fingers,
across the shadow of the house,
silent rubber wheels leaving
tracks in the snow,
footsteps melting into black holes.

We moved into the sun,
sticky as the yellow of an egg.
You, the white-haired old man,
pushing me, the bald-headed baby,
before you in a Taylor Tot.
Round and round we went,
neither of us allowed to cross
the street, tightening the block,
your eyes darting like gray cars
while I scattered bears and Easter bunnies
like seeds along Dodge Street,
Capitol Avenue.

A year, my crazy man,
and I, small duck,
waddled at your side
or came quacking after.
You made bows from the laces
of my shoes, pulled
the nose from my face,

held it between your fingers,
and put it back again.
Pennies, nickels,
grew from your tongue.
Ice-cream cones flowered
from your fists.

Grandpa danced on the roof
with the old army blanket,
and sparks flew like falling stars,
and we all made wishes
as they flew across the parking lot,
flew to the roof
to dance with Grandpa.

And the parking lot lights were on
and the fire truck's lights were on
and the night crouched at our block
like a leopard. His eyes caught
the flame as he watched.

And our eyes caught the flame
and the smoke
and I cried from the sting
and Monsky cried from the sting,
and Lewis cried because he wouldn't sell
any cars in the fall.

And then the horns
trapped inside the cars
began to cry;
the cat crept closer
as the flames disappeared.

Grandma called up
and Grandpa came down
with our army blanket over his arm.

Then the horns trapped
inside the cars died
and Monsky went home
and Lewis went home
and the firemen when home
and all that was left was us

and the cat.

The Flood

> *Crying is active.*
> *The body is in motion.*
> —Ginette Paris

High in the mountains, the heart
begins to melt. Tears gather
in the Lachrymal Lakes, spill
into the Jefferson, the Gallain,
and the Madison that braid
into the Missouri at Three Forks.

They tear through the stockyards
in Sioux City, then race 90 miles
south to Omaha, still a small town,
where, later in the year, I will turn
eight, to blow off sewer covers.

Mother says tears cover 71%
of the earth's surface, comprise
70% of the human body, and
we can not live without them.

My Mother's Wedding

1. She is beautiful, even as the earth cracks
and flames rage. Father Shad steps forward,
parts clouds, draws gold coins from our ears.

Somber witnesses, dark coats pulled tightly
around them, stand as silently as bats hang;
voila, heaven's ruptured; go in peace.

After a great flapping of wings, they sing.
My dress made from thistle taffeta
whistles with every step.

2. Not even tears can grow in this clay.

3. Persephone cries herself to sleep.
Ereshkigal has only to wait.

4. Even in death, the blood red fruit
of the pomegranate rests in a waxy
yellow honeycomb, sweet
delicacy in a hive of love.

5. After the last frost, a thistle shows itself
above ground and a bright prickly star
burns across the dark sandy sky.

6. Night's moon wanes; her rain,
when it falls, falls softly; when the sun
shines, fairies begin to sing.

7. Summer, autumn, winter, spring.

Harvest

Each summer before we moved to the farm,
my stepfather, aided by Miracle Grow,
turned weeds and clay in the vacant lot
behind our house into a productive garden,
where one autumn, my neighbor Mike and I wove
brittle sweet corn stocks into a latticework of walls
and a dome laced with discarded peanut plants
and hybrid pumpkin leaves. At night, we slipped
between the stalks to smoke his mother's cigarettes.
They made us giggle, and dizzy. Then we stretched
side by side on our bed of leaves, ash and cottonwood,
to watch the sky and its stars edging through the sheaves
overhead, and contemplated the days ahead as best
we could with our limited supply of information,
listening to the vesper sparrows settling down,
imagining how, in the morning, we might fly away,
not touching each other for fear we might ignite.

THE CUTTING

The sun has pulled
the dew from the grass,
leaving the roots warm, humid, soft.
The sky is blue, cloudless.
We wait for the breeze.
It comes.

The cutting begins.
I follow my stepfather:
my tractor after his.
The umbrella shades him,
vibrates above his head.
My tractor after his,
my circle inside the circle
of his mower, I trace
the boundary of his last round.
I follow the tire treads
with my eye,
change gears for the first
sharp turns, later follow
rounded corners.

Insects swirl from the grass.
The heat presses up
from the tractor.
The sun shines.
He leads.
I follow, cutting
farther and farther
into the field's center,
until one long swath remains.

He signals and turns to watch.
I circle and approach
as the mower lays the final
grass to rest.

LAVENDER SWEET PEAS

feral in nature,
grew along the fence between
the old and the new farm houses
where I picked a bunch each year
for my mother's birthday,
later for her grave.
She favored their scent. I was taken by
their fine green tendrils intent on escape,
stretching and grasping, hauling themselves
hand over hand across wires and through air,
dragging their lavender satchels
behind them.

BOOK OF FIRSTS

My Father's Voice

"Star detection.
Leave a message.
I'll get back to you."

"STAR DETECTION"

"Star Detection,"
I say to my cat,
and to myself
as I cross Bleecker
to the Grand Union.

"Star Detection,"
I repeat all afternoon,
imagining a man's figure
slouched behind
a steering wheel waiting,
pitching forward
every now and then
as he reaches for coffee,
pistol in pocket,
camera ready, notebook
and pencil beside him
on an empty passenger's seat.

First Interrogation

"Brown," I answer when he calls
with questions. "Dark brown."

"Brown," he answers.
"Dark brown."

"Getting the car doors painted
'Star Detection,'" he explains.

"And picking up stationery,"
he continues, "business cards."

I record this exchange
under the heading "Clue."

My Father's First Letter

1. The Envelope

In the mailroom, a white #7 envelope,
dated, time-stamped, and cancelled
in Omaha, stands on end in my mailbox
displaying his handwriting, I presume,
a jenga stack of ball-point blue--
my full name, correctly spelled,
street address, apartment number,
city, state, zip.

In the upper left-hand corner,
he has written his first name,
middle initial, last name,
his address, Morning Glory Drive,
city, state, zip.

2. The Letter Folded Inside

Under the thick black font
that spells "Star Detection,"
a hollow white pentagram hangs
in the wide clear skies above
Morning Glory Drive.

Beneath the letterhead,
my father's neat cursive
records, in envelope blue,
how he has spent his day.
"Business isn't booming,
yet;" he's following up leads.

He describes my sister,
older by a year,
her husband, and her daughter.
He says she likes to do things
her own way, like getting
married at 18 and having
a baby right away,
and I will like her.

A long time ago, he writes,
he drove a refrigerated truck
carrying eggs into Jersey.
He wasn't home as much
as he wanted; his wife
was some kind of saint.

No one comes near his trailer
when his Akita's outside.
He breeds his dog King
for the pick of the litter.
Do I need protection?

"My dad was Cherokee,"
he writes, "not Sioux;
your great-grandmother
from New York, likely
French Oneida."

I count this letter as half
my chromosomal composition,
each word a gene,
my father made flesh
in the starlight before me.

NOT NECESSARILY BASED
    ON MY FATHER'S DESCRIPTION
    I IMAGINE MY SISTER

Her long red hair glows
in the desert light as she rides
the black horse across the dunes,
the waves of dunes.
Her legs are long; strong,
they hold her to the horse.
The reins lie lightly in her hand.
She hears birds in the Sinai.
When she calls, they stop, listen.
She is the electric of the storm.
She is bronze as an Egyptian coin.
She moves with the wind,
with the shifts of sand.

My sister's eyes, blue as the oasis,
are full of promises.
On her wrists she wears gold bracelets,
sapphire rings on long fingers.
Her breasts are round as melons;
along her back an arrow rides.
My sister takes Bedouin lovers.
Her touch is etched on each
as deeply, as surely, as the morning.

SOME THINGS I KEPT
TO MYSELF FOR A WHILE

My grandmother said my father threatened to steal me
like gypsies stole small children to work carnival
and old Indians once stole stray dogs for supper,

so, she said, my grandfather fashioned the sand box
out back with left-over lumber, a hand-full of shingles,
and a wire fence all around to keep me safe. He

was Indian too, and every Sunday afternoon, he tapped
across the linoleum in black shiny shoes, elbows flexed,
body bent, swaying, singing thanks to the spirits

who gave us all things. She said my father placed the gun
between his lips and pulled the trigger. Imagine
my surprise, Dad, at her door, back from the dead, smiling.

FAMILY STORY

"I tell you," he said that first Christmas,
and never stopped telling as he crossed
the viaduct and turned down Dodge.
Rain melted the gray buildings like flame
melts birthday candles.
"It's something I'll never forget,"
he said, knuckles white on the wheel.

I have not forgotten it either,
not all these years later,
how, he said, his father tracked his mother
down, how police cars parked akimbo in the drive,
how shards of leaded-glass and bits of brain scattered
like Indian corn across the porch,
his parents dead inside.

OUR FIRST GOODBYE

"Your mother was the love of my life,"
he told me on the way to the airport, "the love
of my life," as we crossed the United terminal,

"your mother," he began again and fell silent
at check-in. Upstairs, we waited for the plane,
late from Colorado. "The love of my life,"

he repeated, squinting as though he might find
her hidden behind my eyes, in the shadows
of my cheekbones. Everything's loss, even

the finding, and yet here we were, gathering up
my coat and bag when my flight was called. "Safe
trip home," he said, our embrace awkward.

"Is she happy?" he whispered. "Happy enough,"
I lied, turned back at the jet way to wave goodbye.

FAMILY ALBUM

Hair,
face shape,
clef in the chin,
resemblances are striking
in the photo I took
just after Christmas dinner.

He looks up, startled by the flash,
perhaps puzzled: "How
did the two of us
end up together here?"

Behind him, scattered like distant
stars, lights twinkle on the tree
my grandmother has decorated
each year for as long as I remember.
"Up to you," she wrote,

"whether you meet him,"
announcing his resurrection
and inviting me into a story
in which I had, until then,
a small,
although pivotal,
part.

FIRST WORDS

Finding the right words and using them
are sometimes difficult. I wore the copper bracelet
and practiced calling him "Dad"
even after I returned home
and even when I was alone. I said "My dad"
and "when I visited Dad at Christmas"
and "my dad writes me a letter every week."
"Hello, Dad," when he called.

I tried out the word, "sister,"
circumvented other adjectives and nouns,
"state trooper," "brain matter."

On my kitchen counter, I lined up my vitamins
—ABCs he called them—fastened
the bone necklace he gave me into place,
so as not to dream of ghosts,
locked the ring, its diamonds like stars,
in the safe deposit box, avoided
the verb "love" for as long as I could.

The Sioux City Journal
December 6, 1938

"Kills Divorced Wife and Self,"
a three-column front-page story,
displaced trouble in Italy,
pushed
"Farmer Must
    Lie on 'Barrel'
        For Long Time"
           and
"12,000 Iowans Are
    Sent Federal Income
        Tax Questionnaires"
            below the fold.

            On page six,
with the story jump,
"Pattern 1933,
    Laura Wheeler's designs
        for Church Linen"
      rubbed shoulders with
    "Hearing Notice."

"Lions Plan for
  Annual Christmas
      Party for Blind"
was shoved to one side,
  "Gifts: Sheaffer's Fountain
Pens, Pencils & Desk Sets"
    to the other.

ABOVE THE FOLD,
      AFTER THE JUMP

> There is no poetry in hell.
> --William Packard

Five steps lead up from Sixth Street
to the screened-in porch of the two-story
white frame house where a sign
over the door reads,

GOOD SAMARITAN HOME.

Above the sign, two tall windows, wide
open eyes, overlook the street. The copy
of the newspaper I received is dark. Still
there's a skiff of snow visible in the yard.

The trees are bare: their tapering branches
reach toward the house on this cold
overcast afternoon as though wanting
to warm their fingers. Someone—writer,

photographer, editor—scratched an X
above the top step. This is how far
she got. This is where her body, dead
weight by then, fell through the door.

"TRAGEDY STRUCK"

The front door of the Good Samaritan Home
slammed open.
                    "Get out," Marvin,
the middle son, yelled at his dad.

                         "Get out, get out.
Dad's here," he called to his mother.

His dad "handed him an envelope
                         and drew a revolver."

"You'd better go," Marvin said,
                              then, "Get out,"
again, "as the hammer hit"
"a cartridge failed to explode."

"The boy ran out the back door." His
mother "brushed by the gunman
on her way out the front."

                              "Twice"

the revolver fired.
                    "The shots
hit her in the head."
                         She fell
through the door onto the X someone drew
on the photograph of the front porch,
          822 West Sixth Street.

"The eldest son read the note
later in the day." "I love that woman,"
his dad had written

before he loaded his pistol,
and walked on over.

"NOTE TELLS TROUBLES"

Dear Son,

As I have stood all I can take—

I always said you boys
would never have a stepfather
as long as I lived and not that old tramp.

She has taken all my life from me.

I worked my whole life
for a home and a good bed.
And now she has taken all my life
from me.

All there is left—

Don, I am your father.
She is your mother.
Bury us together in that family lot.

Don, I love that woman. I don't know
why she has done this to me.

Get on your toes, Don, and don't let anybody
take things from you. Save
all you can of my insurance money.

Use it for the baby, God bless his heart.
See that he becomes a man.

Goodbye, Don, Marvin and Lowell.

Dad

PS: My rent is paid until Tuesday night.

REFLECTION

My father, best I can tell from the photograph,
microfilmed then copied, took after his,
eyes, cheekbones, cleft in chin. What

it doesn't show is a man likely to go out gunning
for anyone any time soon (white shirt, faint grin),
although to be honest, that frightens me. "Kills

Divorced Wife and Self," the headline above
reads and the story takes up the front page,
beginning with, "Frustrated by prior attempts

to win back his ex-wife, Alvin wrote a letter
to his eldest son, slipped six shells
into the cylinder of his pistol, paid up
his rent, and went out for one last walk."

MAPS & DESTINATIONS

LES ANGES DECHUS/FALLEN ANGELS

oil, 1833, by F. Cibot

Pugilistic lads with bloodied wings
need their afternoon naps,
which, of course, they refuse to take.

Not so long ago,
they, children from an earlier
marriage, were the favorites.

Listen, shadow boy whispers
to his brother (See the apple
at their feet?), *the soddies*
are a curious lot; they will bite.
He is right, of course; we did.

THE ART OF PAINTING

oil, c. 1666, by J. Vermeer

I rather think him an ass,
the way he's posed me here
with these props—trumpet
stand, laurel wreath, this book
—as though I'm looking over
my own shoulder deep in meditation,
the way he sits all morning
on his own squares looking
and mixing, looking
and marking. "Just there,"
he repeats each time a stray thought
of moon carries me out over the water
or the scent of grass lifts me
onto the new green floor of spring.

Here, the odor of paint and thinner,
the dusty drapes, and clothing oily with use.
Yes, I tap my foot, dry leaves slide,
and my eyes find the window again.
Let him have his art, his black hat,
this room, this fixed time.

Notice he keeps his back to you,
and that in holding me here,
he sets us free to dream.

WOMAN HOLDING A BALANCE

oil, 1662-1663, by J. Vermeer

Here I stand, the *Last Judgment* hanging
over my shoulder, and Christ pointing—
"You go here. You go there."

The poor souls obey
without question.

But notice that I am poised
before the lighted window,
that the scales in my hand are empty,
nothing here, nothing there,
another kind of weighing.

There is never an answer,
only the brush against the canvas,
a trying this, a trying that,
and then the reckoning.

THE LITTLE STREET

oil, 1657-1658, by J. Vermeer

I'm the one in the doorway,
to the right, and this is my favorite time
to mend, morning just greeting cobblestone,
air still chill. Early sun calls us
all outside to wash our walks,
sweep our passageways,
stitch our seams, to start our day
as clean and orderly as the sky,
housekeeping as necessary as vine,
tendrils threading over brick.

IN THE MORNING IN MOROCCO

there are song birds singing
and roosters crowing,
dogs barking and a pneumatic drill
being used on the sidewalk below,
and I wake remembering
these things from Omaha
as if the sound of the sea,
of the gulls were from Omaha, too,
wake wondering that I have traveled
so far to find
dream and reality and dream
just touching at seams
like the panels of heavy curtains
at the window touching,
letting in this bright light
along the edges.

MARRAKESH

This is the red city, the rose city.
Buildings are rose, flat falling sun is rose,
air and sky overhead are rose between
the fingers of the palms.
Listen. Prayers are rose,
rose sent to us through the veins,
generation to generation, to call
from the Kortubia.

Step closer.
The bazaar is every color under the rose sun.
Skin is every color, dye is every color,
rugs every color, the water seller's robe.
Bells ring everywhere. Spices meander
narrow streets. Donkeys pulling carts are every color,
lemon chicken, pigeon pie, those round gray eyes
giving way to black to black-brown. Silk is every color,
brass, but the barber shops are cool blue tile,
cool white tile, always shaded
for fear of the straight razor.

Step into the night,
into indigo folds of loose fitting robes
and tight turbans. Half tones everywhere,
dancers, charmers, snakes and baskets,
and, after the tourists are snug
in their beds, dance. White pants flash like a saber,
like a sword the sword-swallower swallowed.

THE TOURIST

Riding along the Malecón back to the hotel
during the hottest hour of the afternoon,
I watched seawater splash high on the stone

wall ahead and listened to hushed voices
behind me pass time. Then the old Russian
woman we called our ballerina moved

into the seat beside mine. She was slender
as a palm tree, and as graceful. Today,
I cannot give you her name; all I can say

is I was young, that even in tropical heat,
she wore black, that we had never spoken.
My dear, she said softly, slipping her fingers

around my arm, *if we do not love our feet,
our feet will not love us.* Later, as the henna
haired beauticians set to work, our ballerina,

still beside me, praised her misshapen feet,
how they had bled for her without question,
how, at last, they taught her to fly.

TRAVEL PLANS

As I sat on the toilet
of a Boeing 727,
somewhere over Ohio
riding United tourist,
I imagined my last moments
of life
falling bare-assed through the sky,
trying to reach down
to pull up my pants,
then, tumbling,
trying to reach up
to pull my pants down,
so I would land
respectably dressed.

GRAVE RUBBING

1. The child leans into the lobby door waiting,
her cheek against cool plate glass,
her fingers following the canals, each ridge,
vaulted ceilings, spheres, the compass
of flowers deep in the wall covering beside her.

Her eyes attend the lights across the street
where beams of passing cars ricochet
against old oak leaves. Meantime,
her mother starts down the hill.

The girl is only brushed
by hall light. Life lies beyond the six closed
apartment doors, lingers in the corridors,
amid the aroma of pot roast and hash,
baked chicken and liver, potatoes and corn,
peas and baby limas, chocolate cake and apples,
the tincture of burn, the sounds of soft clatter:
chairs bump table legs, shoes rub carpets, small throws,
muffled calls, mute exchanges, radios.

Cigar time: she grows weary.
Black and white tiles spin out cold answers
against her legs.

2. A girl emerges from behind old trees,
later a woman. Determined, she begins a search,
finds angels galore among a battalion of fire fighters,
wings like flames bright in the Havana sun.

Then Mohammed says "Speak only English,
I will show you Tangier." They see *souks*

and the sea. They walk the cemetery corridors,
walled, he says, to keep the spirits in.

The cats have rubbed themselves against the gray
stones of *La Pere Lachaise* so long
they carry inscriptions on their backs.
Old people leave open tins, fish, and cream.

3. She rereads the prairie where the wind
that blows the grass, crumbles
the stones without compassion.
The rain when it does come
has forgotten the names.

She remembers the wall covering.

4. Some days pebbles lead nowhere.
At night, she prays to the mother of stars,
mother of moon,
mother of earth,
wind and water.
The queen of fire-flies answers,
and the queen of painted leaves.
The equator, one fat mama,
belts her heart out.

After a time, her fingers discover
pine, resin as sticky as old blood. Overhead,
each branch holds a secret like a wide umbrella.
So she builds her hut and falls in love with the odor
of cat dander, the deep scent of horse.

5. When the woman returns to the lobby,
her cheek finds the glass,
her hands find the wall,

behind the door, a shard of covering.

There is the fragrance of old wood,
of pot roast and hash, chicken and liver,
potatoes and apples, the tincture of burn.
She imagines the woman starting down the hill.

6. She carries home a piece of wall covering
to study canal and mountain, ridge and sea.

Each flower blooms warm against her skin.

DIALOG WITH SPACE

oil, ca. 1960, by Will Barnet

1.

Imagine huddling on the lip of the horizon
when the sun's just gone down and the rim's still warm.
Imagine the blade of a knife,
the satin edge of a broken fruit jar,
a cool noose.

2.

If the men were to come home,
they would find these women
with the sacred birds.
These are the blackbirds,
those the crows, this a morning dove.
The house has become a weightless place.

3.

She studies the circle
as far reaching as the sea or the prairie.
She notes the cat's green eyes, which,
from where I stand, I cannot see.

THE THREE SISTERS

They, these gray and nameless trees,
stand, hair tossed over their heads
as though caught rinsing it.

I turn to the cherry trees,
raise their white and pink petals,
soft against the hand, but I am back
with the three sisters.
They follow me everywhere—
out of the garden,
down the street,
slide between the sheets,
grow across the page.

Oh these springs are too cold,
too short for us.
No wonder we weep so quickly,
so silently, go about bare
and barren, waiting, preparing
for the first green of summer.

SOMETIMES I IMAGINE
HOW IT MIGHT BE

you and me meeting
in Washington Square
or Piccadilly
like new lovers in old movies.
I imagine it chilly,
yellow with sunlight.
There would be gray pigeons
and children around us,
but I imagine we
would not see them.
I see us run, embrace,
the eyes, the lips.
Then we would walk together,
leg against leg,
delighting in the anxious wait.

WAITING

1975 color lithograph by Will Barnet

I thought there should have been seven,
that I too would have worn a shawl
like the folded wings of the butterfly
against the cold, would have thought my bones
would break in that brittle morning
as I leaned against an opposite beam
and looked past the sand and the sea
to the horizon. I would have said
there was no comfort and that we did not
touch or speak, that it was only the shade
of gray that distinguished us.
We wore our long dark hair parted
and pulled back in a bun.
Perhaps I would have named us
The Poor Widows Waiting at Providence.

Now I even remember this was not
the way it was. There were six
and I was all of them, looking
toward mauve and clear edges,
looking down and away, toward deep recesses.
I was also looking forward.
What I saw, what passed then for grace,
was more than studied composition.
We Women of the Sea did wait,
and when the sun finally warmed us,
we burst into flame.

Moving to Malibu

Some nights I think of it,
moving to Malibu, just as I stretch,
like a cat stretches, to my full length,
as though I am easing into cool waters.
I imagine the blue of the sea;
the bright green leaves of the geranium
on the patio, the bright pink blooms,
the yellow sun and white sand,
in the distance, white triangles,
from the deck, wind chimes.
I will be as content and as happy
as Balboa. I will have breakfast
at my wicker table and in my wicker chair,
with the cats watching. I will taste
salt on my lips after coffee.
My door will be open. When you come,
you will carry a loaf of bread,
a bunch of flowers. The sunset
is brilliant; we might as well be anywhere.

THIS IS BROOKLYN

For Frank

This is Brooklyn
    on a Sunday morning.
 It is summer and the sun shines
 a cool yellow--it is still early.
A breeze comes in the front three windows
        with a sister's voice, no, no, no
        to a younger brother, with a car
        every now and then, the whine
        of wheels. The breeze.
   A breeze comes through the living room where
      I drink coffee, eat a nectarine
        and from where I sat
        until I moved
        I could look through the study
      to the bedroom, to your back,
        the curve of it, gentle rise
       and fall of mountains, no hills,
        golden, burnished in the Sunday
            morning light.
  It is July twenty-second
   of my fortieth year.
  The walls of this room are the color
   of champagne. Brooklyn,
  I have heard it said, is the end
   of the earth. That may be true,
      for at this moment
      that is all there is—
        the breeze, now birds, the yellow
        of the sun, the burnished mountains
            that I will climb.

DAYLILIES

Ruffled Apricot, Master Touch, Grand Finale—
these are the daylilies. They grow everywhere,
here, at Seaview, along side country roads—
School Girl and Joyful Occasion, Cherry Cheeks,
Prairie Blue Eyes. Three years of variation—
Hilled Bandit, Pleasure, and Patterned Gold.

If I were a cat, I would live among them,
among the deep green arches and slender necks.
I would listen to their fine-colored trombones.
A soft bright rain would fall around me.
But I am not a cat. We pin prayer flags
in the backyard trees; red and yellow ribbons
ripple like butterflies in the breeze.
We walk along the beach hunting colorful rocks
and unbroken seashells. Sometimes we swim.

The cat is unconcerned. She watches the bushes,
guards on the back deck what she thinks is hers.
She watches the prayer flags, crouched, with
such intensity that I think she must be praying.
Perhaps she also thinks them butterflies, or birds.
This cat does not yet know daylilies,
although she has appeared in many poems
and in many guises.

Golden Chimes. Banded. This is the first poem
in which my husband appears as my husband,
as in "We pin prayer flags . . ." and
". . . we swim." I pray to the daylilies,
natives of China and far east places.
They are a crisp and lovely magic,
and their flower lives one day through.

Ambrosia and Lemon Lily, they have bloomed,
one on the heels of the last, on Olympus, in Eden,
Joyful Occasion and Patterned Gold,
to this very summer when we hunt colorful rocks
and unbroken shells. Red and yellow ribbons
ripple in the breeze that lifts
the corners of the bright orange flags.
The cat is in her glory. Sometimes we swim.

TRAVEL

Stretched full length on the black and cream sofa
under the green glass ceiling of the third-floor apartment
in overcast Bogotá reading Sarton, *At Seventy*,
I hear the showers begin again. The glass softens;
rain eases its way through, and then we fall together.

We can go anywhere, *Museo del Oro*,
Catedral de Sal Zipequirá, the emerald mines,
coffee fields, hothouses blooming with carnations,
from one continent to the next,
one side of the world
to the next. Water anywhere is water,
blood, blood, another sort of miracle,
this letting go.

After Sightseeing

This is the botanical garden,
although this year there are no orchids
in the orchid capitol of the world,
still very much the Uribe manor it once was,
lakes, woods, lawn, and trees.

This bronze mother and child
pays tribute to *Madremonte,*
this valley our cradle.

A small train circles near,
carrying five- and six-year-olds
who alternate shy and bold.

This is Nora, our guide;
Virginia, our driver, carries our son.

Another mild day,
winter in Medellín; May,
a few leaves fall.

Big boys play basketball
behind the restrooms.
At the garden shop,
starts and clippings and slips.

And there are these little girls
again, at the gate,
snapping on and off like lights,
ready for June,
summer in another hemisphere.

MY DAUGHTER'S WEDDING

In memory of my grandmother

No needle fashioned the hard
gray garment that hangs in marble folds
from the shoulders of the Corn Madonna

chiseled into the altar piece; no backstitch,
blind stitch, cross or feather stitch
holds her robe in place. The stone stare

sees nothing, not the tilt of the earth, not
the priest's chasuble with its appliquéd
chalice and host, not the wedding party,

not the guests, study in dark
and light in their best store-bought
clothes, who arrive like black ice,

not my daughter at the communion rail,
her father who has just stepped aside
to make room for the groom, not the matron

of honor, best man, or even the adolescent girl
whose dress is the color of thistle.
So many rosaries, kernels on a string

to count the days until harvest,
so many bright yellow yolks bud
from the hens we kill for Sunday dinner,

so many dark orbs strung along the deep
fan of the potato's root. When I was eleven

my father hurried each step to the bridge
of the garden fork, plunging the wide tines
into the sandy soil, leveraging earth, exposing
the *pommes de terre*, as he called them, to air.

My job was to pick them up, rub the earth
from their closed eyes. The sky was the color
of my mother's everyday serving platter,

hard as the ground when it freezes.
He said when clouds move east
and Night shakes out her apron,

a swath of bright dust falls to the horizon
where it becomes the moon and rises,
lingers overhead, and then it changes

everything, like the rust on the cloth
between my legs that day. I believe
Night designs her apron, pieced

with running stitch, top stitch, zig-zag
from every place and every person,
every season throughout all time.

MY WEDDING
In memory of my mother

1. My image in the full-length mirror
reflects a middle-aged woman adjusting
her pill box hat and the side seams
of her new navy suit.

                    At the church,
my father—I call him Pop—waits
with my groom and his best man,
not a tux or a smile among them.
The Madonna, sheaf of hard bounty
in her arms, wears gray.

I'd redress everyone somber to light,
except for my thistle girl, perfect
in crinolines and rosy-rust taffeta.

2. My Lady of Nebraska is earth and sky,
plant and animal, birth and death,
sun and moon, flower and weed.

Each spring morning, I smell lilacs,
catch sight of sky, listen to birdsong,
feel the breeze.

3. In her good black gloves, my mother
carries a scroll listing my transgressions,
including the baby, icing on the cake.

4. The tornado picked up the house
the day before I was born
in the corncrib, an omen.

5. The women in my family work hard,
and the men work too and they drink;
they fly into rages, beat their horses
so as not to beat their wives.

6. December's longest day is five days
past. On my way, I saw black ice everywhere.

7. When I close my eyes for the last time,
I will see surprise lilies along the road.

Mountain Figure

Black wax, terra cotta, by Louise Nevelson

1.
I've known nuns who looked like this,
subdued, deep in their robes,
starched into immobility,
neck, head, and bosom,
surplice covering
God's good work.

2.
Even after the war, the Stones
pursued my mother-in-law,
whispering in English
and always coming at night,
stealing food and linens
carrying off pots and pans
up to the attic
just beyond her reach,
just as she was beyond
her children's.

3.
There is a story
about a lonely mountain.
One autumn as trees below
lost their leaves and snow inched
over her shoulders, she coughed out company.
Men and women rolled down the folds
of her skirts and into the valley.
They were not much,
but they were hers, entertaining

even as they rushed about,
learning to speak.
After a time, the mountain seeded
her new skirt with the alphabet.
The women gathering flowers
along its hem also gathered letters.

What's this you've brought us,
the men asked,
when they returned home.
Soon there were children.

4.
The belly of a mountain
forty-nine kilometers north
of Bogotá was emptied
of salt to fashion a cathedral
where penitents still taste salt
on their lips as they pray.

5.
The Northern range of the Andes
is the mother of my children,
their father *Rio Medellín*.
When they slid into our arms,
we sent condors with thanks.

6.
I don long robes to remind
my children of their origins;

the fabric brushes my legs
as I walk the path of nettles
and blooms. Their father tends
the songbirds in the garden
where they play.

WHAT WE KNOW

Paratactic Composition

Chance meeting: moving man
with a truck load of furniture
—beds, chest of drawers, table
and chairs—and a daughter, happy
or ambivalent or, perhaps, pissed.

Sperm, one in millions, dive
bombs a slow moving ovum
and in that free fall, a spark
ignites, burns into the wall,
narrative syntax, my first home.

Grandpa moves up the stairs,
out the heavy swinging door;
I fall away like a discarded coat.

What's the truth? Psyche's task,
one of them, sorting; Aphrodite,
a mother with too much time
on her hands, couldn't leave
well enough alone. Maybe
I was already intent on escape.

"God's paratactic plan," Grandma
might have reasoned, for she was
a seamstress, a woman conversant
in flesh and bone, and transformation.
Later I said *art*; bones break
so we may hear them snap.

LAST RITE

Not my mother coming to the blond brick ranch
house on Ames Avenue one block past the stop
light in the city of my birth to visit the dead.

Everything is modern; each corpse must carry
a zebra stripe hidden on the flip side, this zoo.
Even so, I must say goodbye.

Hello, hello, hello. Right this way.
Do you have an ashtray? My sister and her sister
stand at the coffin with a faintly familiar man.

I notice his wrinkled skin and blue black hair,
think Grecian formula, while our mistress of ceremony,
introduces us: I want you to meet—I want you to meet.

Dad sleeps on. He looks, they say, better,
padded with cotton and complete with false teeth;
I know very well he is not sleeping.

Indian man. Some bury theirs seated,
some they stand straight ready to walk
into the next land. Hello, hello, hello.

I sit between the sisters, and together
we are the gorgons, fates, familiar trinity,
and after the minister speaks, we stand.

When this is over, and the guests go home,
we will hug briefly on Ames Avenue,
go our separate ways.

MAPS AND DESTINATIONS

The Moirae may well be the patron
saints of tapestry and all may be written,
but so much of it is in invisible ink
that when I hold my story to the light,
a fire often flares. I study the ash
like the palm reader off Jackson Square.
My conception on the anniversary
of my grandparents' deaths was, perhaps,
a thread my father cast to pull them back.

Tapestries start with maps, imagined
weavings named cartoons. The Hunt
of the Unicorn's shows each flower;
The Quest for the Holy Grail's holds
narrow shadows in its dark folds.

Even embroidery--French knots, cross
and feather stitches--starts with a plan,
for example, Matilda's bastard tapestry,
the Bayeau linen, on which the Queen
and her Ladies, with eight colors of woolen
yarn, stem-stitched and laid-work history.

Each is planned—The Quest, The Triumph
of Death over Chastity, The Hunt—
a marriage license, the crane's foot
on the treadle of conception, 23 shades
of blue, 23 shades of rose,
father, the warp concealed,
mother, the weft revealed,
and birthed by the beater.

Sanzio's mirror-images survive,

but maps the Moirae fashion perish.
Devoted to their art as though it would last
an eternity, the women moisten
their brushes, touch tip to ash,
draw everything we need:
crane, flower, dog, cat, children.

For example, while I blanket stitch
sky and stubble, French knot small grain,
Lachesis taps time, Clotho spins,
Atropos extends her hand toward the gun.

AN ELEGY

for my mother

I imagine you tilting
forward in your favorite chair;

I had no chance to place
my hand against your cold cheek

before they packed you away,
so I come to you in late winter

to lift you into my arms, stretch your
body out on the living room carpet,

straighten your housecoat, fix your
collar, attempt to put things right,
to say goodbye.

My hands rush to your brow
and my fingers--bold

as they never were before--
trace the flair of each nostril, lips,

note the knoll of each closed eye.
My palms linger at your shoulders

in the manner of your hands upon
the shoulders of my children. I dwell

in the center of you again, trace
your full length, find my way along
the familiar blue trails that crisscross
my own territory. Fields lie fallow.

The moon's past full. Time to wrap
you for the leave taking along the river's
edge where you will desert me once again.

A WALTZ FOR MY MOTHER

Wish I could lift that old gold and white Lira
from the plush red velvet of its case one more time,

guide the wide straps over my shoulders, right, then left,
adjust the bellows over my chest, unsnap the latches

that hold them closed, send the fingers of my left hand
in search of the rhinestone that marks the button C,

and those of my right to the keys to play,
one, two, three, what I called The Bernice Waltz,

to honor my mother on the anniversary of her birth.
Words and chords, notes and rests, all of them lost.

But not the honeysuckle, sounding its golden trumpets
even as the dew clings like tears to the spider's web.

Tonight, lightening bugs blink their songs onto staffs
strung like badminton nets across the lawn;

overhead and within, stars and chromosomes bow
to one another, dance my mother's ghost notes, one, two, three.

The Circle Dance

The great circle dance at the September powwow
is about to begin but
this family has lost a child
over the summer and the grief must be combed
from their hair before they can enter
the circle. The mother walks the grasses
to the west side of the circle. The father
walks the grasses, then the other children,
then the aunts and uncles of this family
who has lost one of its children to accident
over the summer. They stand just outside
the circle, and the old people come with

finger combs and begin running them through
the hair of the family, combing the grief
from the mother, the father, each sister and brother,
aunts and uncles, combing out the grief
like snarls, casting out grief
in tangles. On the north side of the circle,
my scalp tingles. It is grief caught
in my own hair, and I must comb it out
if I am to join the circle. I, too, use my fingers
as a comb, pushing the hair up from the head
and away so the grief can loosen.
This combing takes some time,

and the family begins to cry and the old people,
too, begin to cry, and I on my side of the circle
begin to cry. Tears and grief spill
over my shoulders and run down my legs.
Tears and grief spill over their shoulders
and run down their legs.

The earth receives it as rain, takes it in
as if it were her own because it is her own.
From it she has already begun to fashion
new children to send to us. We
bow to the wisdom of the old people,
enter the circle that we may dance.

WHAT WE KNOW

for Wil and Anna

There is no "side-by-sideness."
--Alfred Schütz

"The Seven Cities of Cibola," my children beg
at bedtime. "Move over," I answer and begin
what is also their story: "Tejo had imagination,
maybe ambition, maybe he just missed his dad,
a trader who set out from time to time to barter
for feathers. Just south of where you two
were born, Guzman heard the words 'gold
and silver forty days away,' remembered
Pizarro in Peru, and organized an expedition."

    The night before my mother's wedding,
    she ran down the hall from the kitchen
    and into her parents' bedroom, two fingers
    against her temples, her mother following,
    repeating: "It's not too late, It's not too late."
    "I have a headache," my mother said in defense.
    Like Guzman standing between four hundred
    Spaniards and twenty-thousand natives,
    I turned and walked out, leaving
    the two women to face each other.

"Estevan the Moor traveled with de Vaca.
Maybe he had imagination or a taste for freedom."

    Several weeks before the wedding, Grandma
    took me to 16th Street for a store-bought dress.
    "We'll cut these off," she said, "so it doesn't look
    cheap." I liked the gold flecks in clear plastic loops
    in the same way I liked painted shells in the aquarium,

the large white hankies she ironed for Grandpa,
and the blue-tiled Russell Stover candy shop
with its slow wheel of hot roasted nuts.

"When Friar Marcos caught up with Estevan,
he was dead. Some say the priest filed conflicting
reports. Others say it is a matter of interpretation."

Grandpa was six feet tall; my uncle, his son,
said he was five-twelve. Mother's new man,
with his shiny black hair and shined brown shoes,
seated at the edge of his seat, was, when he stood,
exactly my mother's height. "He asked me,"
she said, "to marry him. What shall I do?"
Her mother's lips slammed shut like a vault.
Grandpa said, "Eisenhower will be known
for his interstate highways if for nothing else."

"Next Francisco Vasquez de Coronado gave it a shot,
heading north for treasures. He found the Zunis.
Then Alvarado set out. Then Coronado again. *Nada.*"

No snow for Christmas, only the deep cold;
Just after, the wedding, accompanied by sharp winds.
The bride's parents wore black, the groom's black.
I am the girl with pulled back hair, temple pieces
like sharp fins of a fifty-seven Chevy, wearing
a store-bought low-waisted, thistle-colored dress
without pocket decoration, standing outside
the double doors of Our Lady of Nebraska Chapel,
where Mary holds an ear of corn, a sheaf of wheat,
and the couple just exchanged silver.

"Coronado went home; the Indians who survived
planted a little corn and hunted buffalo
for as long as they lasted. *El extremo!*"
  What did Father Shad, the fifth grade religion teacher
  who led them in their vows, know? Or any of us.
  We stood briefly together on a high point of land
  at the side of a church designed to commemorate
  Coronado, a moment in time turned structural.
  My grandparents grew older and died; the couple
  grew old and died; and I sit beside my children,
  descendants of conquistadors, ready for sleep.

PIANO FOUR HANDS

I am the circle
at the end of the dotted line,
geometry of loss
and found, the slip
in the bath tub, the step
from the curb, seed
the carrier pigeon carried off
and the point at which
the river disappears
into the ground.
What if I were to stand
under the wise pine
and not hear the wind?
What if I dropped the stone
and it refused to fall
from my hand? What if,
were I to close my eyes,
I do not open them again?

I could be the circle
at the end of the line,
but instead, by fluke
and necessity, I learned
the art of grafting—
diagonal cuts,
the marriage of
concord and Riesling.
What pleasure the vines,
bent in the sun warming
their old shoulders, hold
after the tap of the first frost.
Our job is not finished.
Listen to the children,
grown now, opening
the bottles one by one,
savoring the gift
of each round hour.

CPSIA information can be obtained at www.ICGtesting.com
Printed in the USA
LVOW07s0924260914

406016LV00006B/8/P